RED SOX RHYMES

RED SOX RHYMES

VERSES AND CURSES

Boston Red Sox Poet Laureate

DICK FLAVIN

wm

WILLIAM MORROW

An Imprint of HarperCollins*Publishers*

HarperCollins books may be purchased for educational, business, or sales promotional use. For information please e-mail the Special Markets Department at SPsales@harpercollins.com.

FIRST EDITION

Designed by Lisa Stokes

Library of Congress Cataloging-in-Publication Data has been applied for.

ISBN 978-0-06-239152-0

15 16 17 18 19   OV/RRD   10 9 8 7 6 5 4 3 2 1

To the memory of Dom DiMaggio, a hero
to a young boy and a role model ever after

CONTENTS

PART VII: FOR THE LOVE OF THE GAME

PART VIII: THE RED SOX AND ME

Like the Olmsted Emerald Necklace and Smuggler's Notch and the Shelburne Museum, Dick Flavin is one of New England's great and unique treasures, albeit one of the region's most animated figures. He has been an Emmy Award–winning television reporter, journalist and satirist, and lo these last few years has become the Fenway Bard because of his poems and lyrics about New England's Olde Towne Team, the Red Sox.

Flavin has recited "Teddy at the Bat" in Boston's Symphony Hall, where Serge Koussevitsky and Charles Munch waved their batons, not to mention followed in the wordsteps of Sherm Feller as the Fenway Park public address announcer—yes, that Sherm Feller, who wrote the 1950s hit "Summertime, Summertime."

His love of baseball and the Townies led him to friendships with Ted Williams, Dominic DiMaggio, Johnny Pesky and Bobby Doerr, and his drive with DiMaggio and Pesky to visit Williams was captured in the late Dave Halberstam's *The Teammates,* the journalist's bestselling book.

Red Sox Rhymes is a wonderful, creative collection of the best of the Bard. Of Hall of Famer Pedro Martinez, he writes, "If a player gave him sass, he'd knock him on his . . ." To celebrate the late autumn signing of Pablo Sandoval, he wrote "Sandoval Is Coming to Town," conjuring images of the Panda dressed as Old Saint Nick.

Flavin's "Roberts Stole That Base" brings back the lore of the most famous steal in Red Sox history, one that set the Red Sox, three outs from elimination, off on a four-game sweep of the Yankees en route to their first world championship since 1918, a steal that landed Roberts in the Red Sox Hall of Fame despite the fact he never had a postseason at-bat in their march to the duck boats. Flavin may well be the only poet to have included Daisuke Matsuzaka's name in an ode, this on the 2007 world championship.

This is about the fun of being a fan, of enjoying the largesse of Williams and Dominic, of El Tiante, Pedro and the Big Schill. There is a place where WAR and OPS+ can be put aside for the simple joy of the game, those who play it and the reasons we watch it. It is about the fortune of growing up around a bunch of other Red Sox, and allowing Dick Flavin to enrich that fortune.

INTRODUCTION

When I was a kid in grammar school I discovered "Casey at the Bat," Ernest Lawrence Thayer's immortal ballad about a star-crossed slugger. Wow, I thought to myself, a poem about baseball. Wasn't poetry supposed to be about the meaning of life, the moon and stars, that sort of thing? This, though, was about a game, one to which I was already addicted. I couldn't get enough of "Casey." Eventually I memorized the whole thing and would recite it at the slightest provocation. Often, to be honest about it, no provocation was needed at all.

When I got to college and would go to the local beer hall with my pals for a few brews, if I ran out of money, which happened as often as not, I would climb up on a chair and loudly recite "Casey" in the hope that someone would take pity on me and buy me a beer. Happily, from time to time the ruse worked.

In ensuing years, as a speaker and television commentator, I learned that writing and speaking in verse could get people's attention and they'd tend to remember more of what I had to say. That's what I did, and still do. But I never completely dropped "Casey at the Bat" from my act. One never gets totally over a first love.

Fast-forward to October of 2001, when I took the road trip of a lifetime for any baseball fan, especially a Red Sox fan, driving by automobile from Massachusetts to Florida with Dom DiMaggio and Johnny Pesky to spend three days visiting with their old teammate Ted Williams, who was gravely ill and in fact dying.

There I was in Ted Williams's living room with three mythic heroes of my boyhood. I had to do something to justify my presence. I decided to do a quick rewrite of "Casey at the Bat" and turned it into a story of the great post–World War II Red Sox teams when DiMaggio batted leadoff, Pesky hit second and the great Williams batted third. I recited "Teddy at the Bat" before an audience of three old men, all of whom have since passed on. I surmised that would be the end of it and that I'd go back to reciting "Casey" in its original form.

When word of our visit got out back in Boston, though, I was more often than not asked to recite my new version of the great old poem that had first appeared in 1888. It was "Casey," not "Teddy," who would be benched.

A few weeks after Ted Williams passed away, the Red Sox held a memorial for him at Fenway Park. It turned out to be the closest thing to a wake or funeral Ted would ever have. They asked me to recite "Teddy at the Bat" before the twenty-five thousand spectators in the stands. It turned out to be the most pressure-packed appearance of my life. But it was also the moment my love for lyric poetry and my love for baseball and the Red Sox came together, and it was a marriage made, if not in heaven, in Fenway Park—

which as far as a lot of Red Sox fans are concerned is just as good as heaven.

I have since written and performed scores of verses on the team and on the game, many of which are in this book. I hope you enjoy reading them—and reciting them, too. And I hope you'll keep in mind that none of them would have happened had not, a long, long time ago, a grammar-school kid discovered and fallen in love with a poem about baseball by Ernest Lawrence Thayer.

PART I

GLORY

For Red Sox loyalists the first sign that the end was at hand for the eighty-six-year march through the barren desert of defeat was almost imperceptible. The Red Sox stood on the brink of being swept by the dreaded New York Yankees in the 2004 American League Championship series. Then in the ninth inning a stolen base by a utility player who would not have even one at bat during that postseason is what lit the fire. That theft led to a game-tying single. Several innings later an extra-inning home run won the game. It was the hit that launched the legend of Big Papi. The next night there was another extra-inning nail-biter, won by a David Ortiz hit. Then came the heroic bloody-sock game followed by a blowout that left the Yankees for dead, at least for that year. The World Series was a joyous victory parade to the Promised Land. The Olde Towne Team ascended to nirvana again in 2007 and, most improbably, in 2013.

Red Sox Nation rediscovered something it hadn't known for more than eight decades. Winning is a good thing.

David Ross and Mike Napoli of the Bearded Brotherhood of 2013.
(Courtesy of the Boston Red Sox.)

THE BEARDS OF SUMMER
c. 2013

In 'oh twelve the Red Sox wound up in last place.

They stunk, but they got themselves back in the race.

In 'thirteen they hit and they threw and they slid.

They won the World Series, that's what those guys did.

They hustled, they bustled, they played hard, they gave.

In fact they did everything except shave.

In springtime, whenever someone hit a double,

You'd notice that on his face was some stubble.

When spring turned to summer there started a buzz.

The more times they won the more fuzz there was.

The season wore on and the pace became brisker;

They kept winning games, sometimes by a whisker.

By the time it was over (this sounds kind of weird),

Just about every guy had a beard.

So now we can say how they got all those wins.

They won by the hair on their chinny-chin-chins.

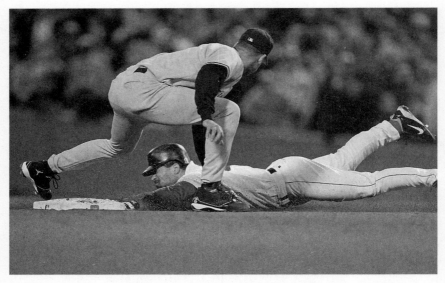

On the brink of elimination by the Yankees in 2004, Dave Roberts steals second base—barely. *(Courtesy of the Boston Red Sox.)*

ROBERTS STOLE THAT BASE

c. 2004

The outlook wasn't brilliant for the
             Beantown nine that night
Down three games to none,
             Ninth inning, end in sight.

So to that stricken multitude
             Ignominy beckoned.
Then pinch runner Roberts
             Made a dash for second.

The catcher came up throwing,
             Jeter raced to take the ball.
Roberts dove. The play was close.
             "Safe!" was the umpires' call.

What happened next will be retold

For years in baseball lore,
For that theft sparked a comeback
Unheard of before.

Mueller singled Roberts home
And several innings later
Big Papi put the game away
With a home run 'tater.

The Sox went on to win game five,
Game six and then game seven.
The Yanks were dead. The Cards got swept.
And hello, Baseball Heaven.

There was cheering there was singing,
And heroes filled the place.
But it never would have happened
Had not Roberts stole that base.

Two hundred forty thousand fans per year tour Fenway
Park. *(Memorabilia from the Collection of Richard Johnson.)*

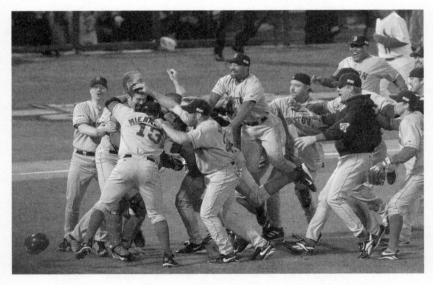

October 27, 2004, Busch Memorial Stadium, St. Louis. The curse is reversed! *(Courtesy of the Boston Red Sox.)*

THE RED SOX RAZZLE-DAZZLE

(To the tune of "Razzle-Dazzle" from the musical Chicago)

c. 2004

We gave 'em the old razzle-dazzle

We razzle-dazzled 'em

We started out by sweeping Anaheim

Then it was on to crush-the-Yankees time

Gave 'em a full three-game head start

Then we clobbered 'em

How could they win with A-Rod's girly slap?

The Empire choked and it was shocking

With Damon's hair and Schilling's stocking

We razzle-dazzled 'em

And now we're on the map

We gave 'em the old razzle-dazzle

We razzle-dazzled 'em

We finished up against St. Louis

Four games later they were singin' the blue-iss

Gave 'em the old eight-game win streak

Stunned and staggered 'em

And that World Series flag is now unfurled

Red Sox Nation is all in clover

And here is why—the Curse is over

We razzle-dazzled 'em

Now we're champs of the world!

A Red Sox Christmas card.
(Memorabilia from the Collection of Richard Johnson.)

2013 was a Red Sox Christmas to remember.
(Courtesy of the Boston Red Sox.)

A RED SOX CHRISTMAS STORY
c. 2013

'Twas the night before Christmas and all through the park
Not a creature was stirring, the whole place was dark.

The season was over and in the grandstand
I was sitting alone; there was no other fan.

When up on the Wall there arose such a clatter
I sprang from my seat to see what was the matter.

And what should appear as if in a dream
A Red Sox manager and a whole baseball team.

He had a square jaw and a chest like a barrel.
I knew in a moment it must be John Farrell.

Then, giving a nod to the famed pitcher's mound,
Down the Fisk Pole the manager slid with a bound.

He was wearing his uniform and on his back
He carried a bundle of gifts in a sack.

He crept to the infield and from the bag took
A gift so amazing my whole body shook.

It was for the children, Mom, Dad and Aunt Sophie

For, lo, I beheld the World Series Trophy.

It glittered and glowed and made everything bright

And no one had even turned on any light.

Gently he held it with tenderness great.

Then he carefully placed it right there on home plate.

And raising his hand to the bill of his hat

Up the Fisk Pole he rose as quickly as that.

Back to the players he hustled his way

And he called out to them as he jumped in his sleigh,

"On Lester, on Lackey, on Shane Victorino,

Off we shall fly in the name of Lucchino.

On Koji, on Buchholz, Pedroia and Gomes,

We're flying tonight to Sox Nation homes."

And I heard him exclaim as he flew with those jocks,

"Merry Christmas to all from the Boston Red Sox!"

A THIRST FOR FIRST
c. 2013

Larry, you got us the championship,
God bless you and we think you're swell.
But let us be clear, if we don't win next year,
We're going to be madder than hell.

That's three in ten years; hallelujah and cheers!
You've caused us to dance and to sing.
But, Larry, we mean, since twenty thirteen
You haven't won a damn thing.

You've brought us home first, but you've unleashed a thirst
That is common to each Red Sox nut.
Now we want even more or else we'll be sore,
Which is why we're a pain in the butt.

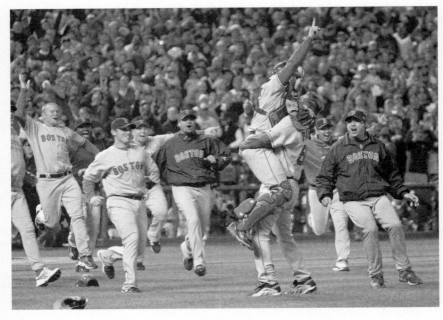

2007—the Nation's team does it again.
(Courtesy of the Boston Red Sox.)

THE NATION'S TEAM
c. 2007

They're from as nearby as Hyde Park,
        Japan so far away,
Puerto Rico, the Dominican
        And across the USA.

They represent each one of us,
        Each color, shape and size.
But together they're one unit.
        That's how they won the prize.

On the mound are Josh and Wake,
        The Big Schill and Dice-K.
And young arms like Jon Lester
        And Buchholz, first name Clay.

Okajima's in the pen,
        He always comes up big
To close it out Jon Papelbon
        Will do an Irish jig.

With Big Papi, Varitek and Youk
> There's no way we'd go wrong.

And J. D. Drew and Lugo,
> They both finished strong.

Mike Lowell comes through in the clutch
> So often it's uncanny.

Coco's flying through the air,
> And Manny's being Manny.

And what about the future?
> It looks good even there.

Pedroia's safe at second.
> Ellsbury's everywhere.

They fought the fight. They stayed the course.
> They brought us jubilation.

They won the championship for us.
> They won for Red Sox Nation.

So let us all salute them,
> They've fulfilled our dream.

All hail the Boston Red Sox,
> All hail the Nation's Team!

THE RIDE OF THE RED SOX
c. 2004

Listen, my children, you fans and you jocks,
To the championship ride of the Boston Red Sox.
It's the nineteenth of April in two thousand four,
And we're off on a ride that will go down in lore.

We've got Pedro and Schilling and Derek and Tim,
And the Damn Yankees' hopes already look dim.
There is Damon and Manny and Kevin Millar,
Bill Mueller and Pokey, each one an all-star.

Varitek catching will lead the attack,
As for Nomar and Nixon, they're both coming back.
And this is why we're reciting this verse,
In two thousand four we will bury the curse.

We'll stamp out the Yankees and win in the East,
And the playoffs will be a great victory feast.
And when that World Series flag is unfurled
It will say, "Boston Red Sox, the Champs of the World!"

Jubilation comes to Fenway Park.
(Courtesy of the Boston Red Sox.)

YOU'RE THE SOX

(To the tune of "You're the Top")

c. 2007

You're the Sox
You're the Series winner
You're the Sox
You're a champagne dinner
    You're a three-base hit
    Mirabelli's mitt
    You're bliss
You're a prime-time Emmy
You're Jerry Remy
You're Youkilis

You're the dome
On the great Francona
You're a comb
    He is not the owner
    He has got no hair
    But we don't care
    He rocks

And you brought home that trophy
You're the Sox!

You're the Sox
You're a Beckett heater
You're the Sox
You're a Yankee beater
  You're Jon Papelbon
  When he comes on
  To save
He'll soon be jigging
But first he's digging
A hitter's grave

You're the bling
On an Ortiz buckle
You're the ring
On Tim Wakefield's knuckle
  You're the microphone
  When Castiglione
  Just talks
And you brought home that trophy
You're the Sox!

You're the Sox
You're Ellsbury running
You're the Sox
You're Curt Schilling's cunning
 You're a long, long fly
 You're a curveball by
 Dice-K
You're the next on deck
You're Varitek
A triple play

You're the pole
For which Pesky's noted
You're Mike Lowell
An all-star you're voted
 You're Lucchino's brain
 You're Manny's mane
 Those locks
And you brought home that trophy
You're the Sox!

You're the Sox
You're John Henry's money

You're the Sox
You're the Easter Bunny
        You're the infield dirt
        On Pedroia's shirt
        Each game
You're a ballpark yell
And you can spell
Yastrzemski's name

You're the stretch
In the seventh inning
You're the catch
That'll keep us winning
        You're a team that's proud
        To whom the crowd
        Just flocks
And you brought home that trophy
You're the Sox!

Boston Globe headline from 1918. We'd wait eighty-six years to see another. *(Memorabilia from the Collection of Richard Johnson.)*

The World Series Trophy, baseball's Holy Grail.
(Courtesy of the Boston Red Sox.)

THE TROPHY
c. 2013

Bring on the magic. Trot out the reward,
The prize for all of those runs that we scored.

It's the Oscar, the Emmy, all rolled into one;
It's Big Papi's earring, the moon, stars and sun.

It's the end o' the rainbow, our own pot of gold.
It's three in ten years but it never gets old.

It's the highest of honors. Above all it towers,
It's the World Series trophy, and by God it's ours!

I've got a ring. Don't tell Larry.
(Courtesy of the Boston Red Sox.)

THE RING
c. 2013

My God, I've got a Series ring.
>> Please, do not wisecrack.
If Lucchino hears about this
>> He'll make me give it back.

I am not a home run hitter,
>> Don't have a great curveball;
I run real slow and I can't throw
>> And I don't play at all.

I'm the designated dreamer.
>> I think up funny rhymes.
I sit up in the PA booth,
>> At least I do sometimes.

I really must be going now.
>> I do not dare to linger.

Larry will take back the ring
    And then give me the finger.

You want to know how I got this,
    This bauble that I wear?
All right, this is the honest truth—
    I stole it, fair and square.

PART 2

TRAIN WRECKS

The agony and the ecstasy" is a phrase that describes the highs and the lows of sports competition. For Red Sox fans it's more like the ecstasy of the agony. The team groveled in despair for so long that its fans came to embrace the pain of it. They wore their defeats and disappointments like badges of honor. They reveled in their wretchedness.

But the Sox have now won it all not once but three times, and if the disasters don't seem quite as earthshaking, fear not. The Red Sox have not forgotten the fine art of dashing the hopes of their acolytes. Rooting for the Red Sox has become somewhat different, though. Where it used to be all about wallowing in splendid misery, it has morphed into an emotional roller-coaster ride of worst to first and back to worst again. So the rule still applies; if you like a good train wreck, follow the Red Sox. Sooner or later you'll see one.

Every Red Sox fan learns early that not all stories end happily ever after. *(Courtesy of the Boston Red Sox.)*

A RED SOX PRAYER
c. 2014

Oh, Dominic, Pesky, Williams and Stephens,

Please, Lord, protect us from Damn Yankee heathens.

They torture us, beat us, and that's just for starters.

And we're sick of being the Bronx Bomber martyrs.

They're devils in pinstripes, dear Lord, even worse,

So to you we pray in this poor, humble verse.

You've performed miracles, done it before,

Just look what you did back in two thousand four.

Then you did it again in two thousand seven.

You answered our prayers up in baseball heaven.

And you brought back the act in twenty thirteen.

What a crowd pleaser, Good Lord, really keen.

For that we thank you and we praise you greatly,

But, God, you haven't done much for us lately.

THE ROLLER COASTER
c. 2013

Rooting for the Olde Towne Team
      Has twists and turns to make one scream.
It's not a simple, easy glide.
      It's like a roller-coaster ride.
It takes you to the very top.
      My God, you're in a nosedive drop!
A look of panic's on your face
      You plummet right into last place.
You careen at breakneck speed.
      Then your nose might start to bleed.
You hold on tight, you're one scared pup.
      Then you think you might throw up.
Then once again you're back on top.
      Then comes another belly flop.
The ride gives you the Red Sox bends,
      And worst of all it never ends!

THEY'RE COMING AFTER US

c. 2002

They're coming after us, gang,
       They're coming after us.
The Red Sox killed our fathers
       Now they're coming after us.
They draw us in each season,
       Win our undying trust.
And then they break our hearts, gang.
       Our hopes all turn to dust.
A muffed ground ball, an ump's bad call,
       An innocent pop fly,
A manager's decision
       Can make a grown man cry.
When vict'ry seems within our grasp,
       When ev'rything's a plus,
That's when we should brace ourselves.
       They're coming after us.

Harry Frazee, the man who sold Ruth to the Yankees. Thanks a lot, Harry. *(Courtesy of National Baseball Hall of Fame Library, Cooperstown, NY.)*

THAT'S HARRY FRAZEE

(To the tune of "Peggy O'Neill")

c. 2003

Harry Frazee was a son of a bee.

The worst one in hist'ry he ranks.

I'll tell you why, because he was the guy

Who sold off Babe Ruth to the Yanks.

If he sold his soul for gold, that's Harry Frazee.

If the Yanks took Ruth with thanks, that's Harry Frazee

If he gave them our whole pitching staff,

If he gave to the Red Sox the shaft,

He's burning in hell, of course.

We think that's swell, of course.

That's Harry Frazee!

If he trashed the team for cash, that's Harry Frazee.

If he bled the town then fled, that's Harry Frazee.

If he took every cent he could get

Then tried to blame it on No, No, Nanette,

He's burning in hell, of course.

We think that's swell, of course.

That's Harry Frazee!

Chick Stahl, the only Sox skipper who never got fired.
(Courtesy of the Boston Red Sox.)

CHICK STAHL

c. 2006

Are you one of those wise guys,
   Those blowhards, those jocks,
Who thinks you can manage
   The Boston Red Sox?
Well, it's not all that easy,
   Oh no, not at all.
Just take, for example,
   The case of Chick Stahl.
Chick managed the Red Sox
   In nineteen oh-six,
But the fact the team stunk
   Put Chick in a fix.
Next year in spring training
   They still couldn't win.
So Chick took bold action.
   He did himself in.

The boo-birds that season
>Would not get to Chick.

Carbolic acid
>Is what did the trick.

He gulped the stuff down
>And quickly expired,

The only Sox skipper
>Who never got fired.

So, should the position
>Become yours to fill,

Before you accept it
>Please make out your will.

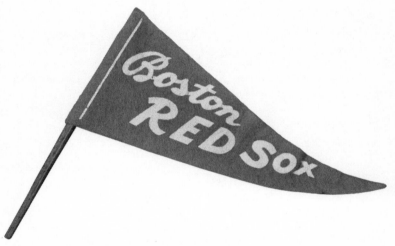

There was a time when Red Sox pennants were rare.
(Memorabilia from the Collection of Richard Johnson.)

A bad day at the office for the Olde Towne Team.
(Courtesy of National Baseball Hall of Fame Library, Cooperstown, NY.)

THE RED FLOPS SONG

(To the tune of "Charlie on the MTA")

c. 2011

Let me tell you the story
Of a team from Boston
In a tragic and fateful year
They led the league all season
Then for some strange reason
Wound up crying into their beer.

    Did they finish the race?
    No, they were a disgrace.
    At flopping they were tops.
    The revolting news is
    That the bums were losers,
    The two thousand eleven Red Flops.

They drank beer in the dugout
And they ate fried chicken
And the pitching really stunk

And the losses were plenty
They went seven and twenty
And the whole damn season was sunk.

(Chorus)

In the month of September
They just couldn't remember
How to be half-decent players.
And it needn't be stated
They were well compensated.
They were multimillionaires.

(Chorus)

The meltdown that transpired
Got the manager fired
And that's a well-known fact
And although it's not funny
They got paid all that money
For a disappearing act!

(Chorus)

THE GOOD OLD DAYS

(To the tune of "Those Were the Good Old Days,"
from the musical Damn Yankees)

c. 2008

I see Billy Buckner bending
And all our hopes are ending.
  The ball is rolling through
  His legs before our gaze.
And that horrible truth
When we learned they sold Ruth
  Those were the good old days.

I see Bucky Dent of all guys
The weakest of the small guys
  That cheesy little homer
  Floating through the haze.
And my heart is at risk
They forgot to sign Fisk
  Those were the good old days.

I know it's not pretty to wallow in pity
There's nothing of value one can gain.
Then all of a sudden I see Don Buddin
And again I'm awash in wondrous pain
    (Is anybody happy?)

I see Grady Little snoring
While Yankee runs are scoring
    Pedro's out of gas
    But in the game he stays
And there's Slaughter's mad dash
Another late-season crash
    Those were the good old days

Oh I'd complain and I'd beef
But I miss the grief
    Of those good old days.

PART 3

THE LYRIC
LITTLE BANDBOX

John Updike, in his famed *New Yorker* essay "Hub Fans Bid Kid Adieu," described Fenway Park as a "lyric little bandbox," causing people to consider for the first time that the old yard was perhaps more than just a conglomeration of curious measurements and quirky angles.

The park is dominated by the Green Monster, the infamous thirty-seven-feet-high left-field wall that looms, seemingly, just beyond third base. The Pesky Pole in right field is just three hundred two feet down the line, the shortest distance in major league baseball, yet the configuration of the stands is such that Fenway's right field is the largest in major league baseball. Five hundred two feet away from home plate, deep in the blue seats of the bleacher section, is a single seat that is painted red. It marks the spot where, on June 9, 1946, Ted Williams hit the longest home run in the place's history.

In a city filled with historic tourist attractions, Fenway Park is the most popular of them all. It pulsates with game-day action and it resonates with history. It is, in Charles Steinberg's phrase, America's most beloved ballpark.

Fenway Park—baseball's great crown jewel.
(Courtesy of the Boston Red Sox.)

LONG LIVE FENWAY PARK
c. 2012

For a hundred years she's stood here,
     Heard cheering, seen our tears;
Through all the good times and the bad
     Fenway perseveres.

She's baseball's great crown jewel,
     A treasure—this is why.
Look out there on her field, you'll see
     The ghosts of games gone by.

There's Babe Ruth standing on the mound,
     Ted Williams at the plate.
And someone's great-grandfather
     Just came in through the gate.

That's Yaz patrolling in left field,
     In center, Freddie Lynn;

Cronin's playing shortstop
>   But Pesky's coming in.

Luis Tiant whirls and spins
>   And then he lets it go.
There's another leaping catch
>   By Dom DiMaggio.

Jim Rice lines one off the wall,
>   Malzone comes in to score.
Pedroia makes a diving stop,
>   Or is that Bobby Doerr?

Fisk hits one deep into the night.
>   Will it be foul or fair?
It caroms off the foul pole
>   And the cheers still fill the air.

Dewey Evans's rifle arm
>   Just cut a runner down.
There's Tony C., still young and strong,
>   The toast of his hometown.

Roberts steals another base
    Pinch running for Millar.
There's Radatz, Lonborg, Jimmie Foxx,
    And Pedro and Nomar.

Look closely. You can see them all.
    They come here every day.
Fenway was and is their home.
    It's where her ghosts still play.

And in the dugout by first base,
    There sits the current squad.
Someday they will take their place
    With all the Fenway gods.

That's why this place is magic,
    Why she's made such a mark.
She's a hundred plus and going strong.
    And long live Fenway Park!

The sights and the sounds of Fenway Park.
(Courtesy of the Boston Red Sox.)

SIGHTS AND SOUNDS
c. 2011

It's the roar of the crowd. It's the crack of the bat.
It's all those folks wearing their favorite team's hat.
It's the kid selling hot dogs, the guy sipping beer,
The stands filled with people just waiting to cheer.
It's the fan with the scorecard she's ready to mark.
It's the sights and the sounds of the park.

It's the grass in the outfield, an umpire's call;
It's the Green Monster seats on the top of the wall.
It's the scoreboard in center, the foul pole in right,
The road team in gray and the Red Sox in white.
It's an infielder diving, a home run's great arc.
It's the sights and the sounds of the park.

There's no place quite like it, you know when you're there.
You see it; you hear it; feel it in the air.

It's the throng in the bleachers, a hit down the line.

It's singing and swaying to "Sweet Caroline."

It's a thousand lights shining. It glows in the dark.

It's the sights and the sounds of the park.

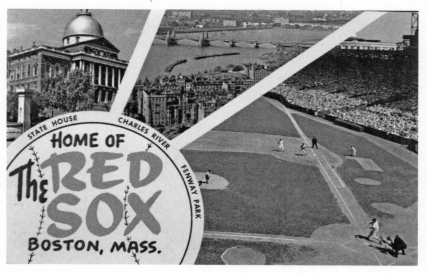

Three landmarks—the Statehouse, the Charles River, and Fenway Park. *(Memorabilia from the Collection of Richard Johnson.)*

The trees on Yawkey Way have been there longer than the ballpark. *(Courtesy of the Boston Red Sox.)*

THE TREES
c. 2005

Outside of Fenway there's a tree.
Or, more precisely, there are three.
And they all have a history.
They're older than both you and me.

They were there before Babe Ruth,
Before the ballpark, that's the truth.
That means they're lengthy in the tooth,
Forsooth, no longer in their youth.

Next time you're out on Yawkey Way
And buy a sausage, let us say,
If it's been there as long as they
You'll take a bite, and then—oy vey!

Opening Day, 2009—Ted Kennedy throws the ceremonial first pitch. It was his last public appearance in Boston. *(Courtesy of the Boston Red Sox.)*

TEDDY ON THE MOUND
c. 2009

The outlook wasn't sunny for the Red Sox Opening Day,
It got rained out and Beantown fans would wait until Tuesday.
But that loyal multitude was sure to hang around,
They knew it would be worth the wait with Teddy on the
      mound.

The moment came, from deep left field the crowd let out a roar
It rattled in the mountains and echoed from the shore.
The cart in which he rode was just enveloped by the sound
For Teddy, our own Teddy, was advancing to the mound.

There was shouting, there were cameras, there was glamour,
      there was glitz
The old park hadn't felt this way since dear old Honey Fitz.
When he stepped out of the cart the cheering shook the ground

No stranger in the crowd could doubt 'twas Teddy on the
    mound.

There was ease in Teddy's manner and a smile on Teddy's face,
Then he took the ball in hand and Jim Rice took his place.
Great Teddy leaned into the plate as he got set to throw,
And now the crowd grows hushed and still, and now he lets it go.

Oh somewhere in this land of ours the sun is shining bright,
The band is playing somewhere, and somewhere hearts are light
And Teddy's fans are happy, because, what's not to like?
It took one hop to get there, but Teddy threw a strike!

THE SELLOUT STREAK

c. 2013

Seven hundred nine four in a row

That is a sellout record, you know.

But Fenway's streak went suddenly dark

Once I took the mike at the old park.

My lilting voice affects folks that way.

When people hear it they stay away

The place was jam-packed for that first game

But the next game attendance was lame.

Six thousand fewer showed up for game two,

Not a good omen, not in my view.

At that rate Fenway, this is no lie,

Could be a vacant lot by July.

The left field wall, Fenway's great Green Monster.
(*Courtesy of the Boston Red Sox.*)

SHE'S A GRAND OLD WALL

(To the tune of "You're a Grand Old Flag")

c. 2014

She's a grand old wall,
Thirty-seven feet tall,
With a scoreboard that functions by hand.
She's got seats on top
Looming over shortstop,
A view that's the best in the land.
She's a great landmark
Dominating the park,
The most famous in all baseball.
The great Green Monster of Fenway Park,
There's none like her, that grand old wall.

She's a grand old wall
And she never will fall

Although walloped by many line drives.

She gives up home runs,

Two-base hits by the tons.

She also gives pitchers the hives.

For she seems so near

She instills them with fear.

If they should give up a fly ball

And it's hit real high, kiss it good-bye,

'Cause it's over that grand old wall.

PART 4

TEDDY AND THE TEAMMATES

Ted Williams had an animal magnetism about him that was as powerful as it was unique. Johnny Pesky captured it best when he said, "It was like there was a star on top of his head, pulling everyone toward him like a beacon." It was true, as anyone who was ever in Williams's presence can attest. His God-given talent, his demonic work ethic and the wattage of his charisma set him apart.

But he looked to others for leadership. In the early days it was Bobby Doerr, who was so balanced and even tempered, to whom the tempestuous young Ted turned for guidance. In later years, it was Dom DiMaggio, who had achieved such success beyond baseball in both business and his personal life, who emerged as the leader. Pesky, just a little younger than the others, always considered himself, even when he was in his eighties, to be the little brother. Together they formed the core of the great Red Sox teams of the post–World War II era.

In the years following their playing careers, as their lives took different twists and turns, they never stopped caring for each other. They were teammates to the end.

And now the air is shattered by the force of Teddy's blow.
(Courtesy of the Boston Red Sox.)

TEDDY AT THE BAT

(With apologies to Ernest Lawrence Thayer)

c. 2001

The outlook wasn't brilliant for the Red Sox nine that day,
The score stood four to two with but one inning left to play.
So when Stephens died at first and Tebbetts did the same
A pallor wreathed the features of the patrons of the game.

A straggling few got up to go, leaving there the rest
With the hope that springs eternal within the human breast.
They thought if only Teddy could get a whack at that.
They'd put even money now with Teddy at the bat.

But Dom preceded Teddy and Pesky was on deck.
The first of them was in a slump. The other was a wreck.
So on that stricken multitude a deathlike silence sat,
For there seemed but little chance of Teddy's getting to the bat.

But Dom let drive a single, to the wonderment of all,
And Pesky, of all people, tore the cover off the ball.
When the dust had lifted, and they saw what had occurred,
There was Johnny safe on second and Dominic on third.

Then from that gladdened multitude went up a joyous yell,
It rumbled in the mountains and rattled in the dell.
It struck upon the hillside and rebounded on the flat,
For Teddy, Teddy Ballgame, was advancing to the bat.

There was ease in Teddy's manner as he stepped into his place,
There was pride in Teddy's bearing and a smile on Teddy's face.
And when, responding to the cheers, he lightly doffed his hat,
    (I'm making that part up)
No stranger in the crowd could doubt 'twas Teddy at the bat.

Ten thousand eyes were on him as he rubbed his hands with dirt,
Five thousand tongues applauded as he wiped them on his shirt.
Then when the writhing pitcher ground the ball into his hip,
Defiance gleamed in Teddy's eyes, a sneer curled Teddy's lip.

And now the leather-covered sphere came hurtling through the
    air,
And Teddy stood a-watching it in haughty grandeur there.
Close by the sturdy batsman the ball unheeded sped.
"That ain't my style," said Teddy. "Strike one!" the umpire said.

From the benches black with people went up a muffled roar,
Like the beating of the storm waves on the stern and distant
    shore.
"Kill him! Kill the umpire!" someone shouted on the stand,
And it's likely they'd have killed him had not Teddy raised his
    hand.

With a smile of Christian charity great Teddy's visage shone.
He stilled the rising tumult and bade the game go on.
He signaled to the pitcher, and once more the spheroid flew.
But Teddy still ignored it, and the umpire said, "Strike two!"

"Fraud!" cried the maddened thousands, and the echo
    answered, "Fraud."

But one scornful look from Teddy and the audience was awed.

They saw his face grow stern and cold, they saw his muscles
strain,

And they knew that Teddy wouldn't let that ball go by again.

The sneer is gone from Teddy's lip; his teeth are clenched in
hate.

He pounds with cruel vengeance his bat upon the plate.

And now the pitcher holds the ball, and now he lets it go,

And now the air is shattered by the force of Teddy's blow.

Oh, somewhere in this land of ours the sun is shining bright,

The band is playing somewhere, and somewhere hearts are
light,

And somewhere men are laughing, and somewhere children
shout.

And they're going wild at Fenway Park 'cause Teddy hit one
out!

I KISSED TED WILLIAMS

c. 2009

I kissed Ted Williams on the cheek,

Oh, I admit that he was weak

And pretty old, in fact, antique

When lips I puckered up to seek

To plant that peck upon his cheek.

How many of us can so speak?

Well, countless women, fair and sleek,

And me, one funny-looking geek,

Have kissed Ted Williams on the cheek.

We could have formed a club, a clique,

The girls and I, we'd be quite chic.

I have to say sometimes I shriek.

If Teddy had been at his peak

When that small smooch I sought to sneak

He would have thrown a fit of pique

And whacked me squarely on the beak,

Then knocked me right into next week.

He'd go too far, that's my critique.

Me? I'd have turned the other cheek.

July 12, 1943—the Kid and the Babe on the day of their home run hitting contest. (© *Ted Williams Family Enterprises, Ltd., reproduced by permission.*)

TED VS. BABE

c. 2010

On the twelfth of July many decades gone by,
Forty-three was the year long ago,
This happened, the truth, Ted Williams, Babe Ruth,
Faced off, bat to bat, toe to toe.

Fenway Park was the spot where the battle was fought,
At home plate, believe it or not.
This was the great test, which one was the best.
The Kid or the Sultan of Swat?

Ted was just twenty-four. He had gone off to war,
But was brought back for the big day.
The Babe, twice as old, but nonetheless bold,
Was positive he'd have his way.

For a charity game all-stars of great fame
From the military were there.

Ted was just one who'd join in the fun.
On hand to greet all was the mayor.

And up from Broadway came Ruth for the day
But the game would take a backseat
When an idea was hatched, a home run hitting match,
The Kid and the Babe would compete.

First up was the Kid and here's what he did,
Ten swings, three into the seats.
On Babe's second swing he fouled off the thing,
Hurt his foot and conceded defeat.

Then in the game Ted homered again
The Babe couldn't stand to lose face.
But at age forty-eight he was no longer great
And he popped out to second base.

For one day, at least, the argument ceased.
Yankee fans, we hope you're not hurt,
But let it be said, if you bet against Ted,
Then you, I'm afraid, lost your shirt.

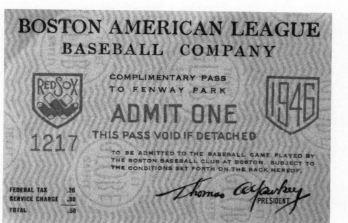

A VIP pass from 1946.
(Memorabilia from the Collection of Richard Johnson.)

September 28, 1940—Ted's last blast in his last at bat.
(Courtesy of the Boston Red Sox.)

WERE YOU THERE?
c. 2013

Were you there the day of Ted's last blast?

Were you part of his supporting cast?

Were you fully grown or just a tyke?

Were you sitting next to John Updike?

A million people say they were,

But the records don't concur.

There were just ten thousand in the stands,

Whooping, cheering, clapping hands.

Are you sure you're right to make such claims?

Or is your mem'ry playing games?

Some on their mothers' graves have sworn,

Even though they weren't yet born.

A million fans plus you were there?

That's more than showed up all that year.

Perhaps you're fudging just a bit.

In fact, I think you're full of sheer enthusiasm for Ted Williams.

Ted Williams, center, Jimmie Foxx, right, and an unidentified teammate in the late thirties. Those were the days. *(Courtesy of the Boston Red Sox.)*

THOSE WERE THE DAYS

(A parody of the theme song from All in the Family*)*

c. 2005

Boy, the way that Pesky played
What a bunch of hits he made
Damn it, he was underpaid
Those were the days.

Pitching, as a rule it stunk
Septembers all our hopes were sunk
The manager was usually drunk
Those were the days.

Dominic and Bobby Doerr
Think of all the runs they'd score
What the hell was Denny Galehouse
In that playoff game for?

Teddy Williams and his bat
Fenway Park was where it's at
Birdie Tebbetts's bum was fat
Those were the days.

Dom DiMaggio, the Little Professor. Put him in the Hall!
(*Courtesy of National Baseball Hall of Fame Library, Cooperstown, NY.*)

THE LITTLE PROFESSOR
c. 2003

A player must be worthy to be in the Hall of Fame.

It must be clear he has the stuff by how he played the game.

Three ways there are to measure him that cannot be ignored;

One is hitting, two is fielding and three is runs he scored.

At each of those one man stood out, that's why we should
    bestow

Enshrinement in the Hall of Fame on Dom DiMaggio.

In the years he played he had more hits than any other man.

He had more doubles than them all, except for Ted and Stan.

Look up all the runs he scored because they clearly state

That Dom trailed only Williams in times he crossed the plate.

When he was out in center field, that's where Dom excelled.

And the proof is in the records that he set and held.

His chances and putouts per game over a career—

Records that he holds today—stand up every year.

He set single-season records back in nineteen forty-eight

But for expansion they'd still stand. In the outfield he was great

And if all that were not enough, here's still another reason:
One hundred runs he averaged, that's what he scored per season.
The only man to do that who's not now in the Hall,
Surely he deserves to have his plaque upon the wall.
Dom DiMaggio, great player, credit to the game,
And, as a man, we'll tell you this, he's in our the Hall of Fame.

1946 World Series ticket.
(Memorabilia from the Collection of Richard Johnson.)

Johnny Pesky, Mr. Red Sox.
(Courtesy of the Boston Red Sox.)

FAREWELL, JOHNNY
c. 2012

Here's to you, Johnny Pesky,
    You're baseball in this town.
You played. You coached. You managed.
    You never let us down.

Two hundred hits a season
    When you played, how's that?
You hold the all-time record
    For swings with a fungo bat.

They named a foul pole after you.
    The reason, it is clear,
Is you could hit the ball that far—
    Once or twice a year.

You saw them all, from Ted and Dom
    To Yaz, Big Papi, too.

Seventy years of players
    All learned a thing from you.

You're Mr. Red Sox. You're the man!
    You're in our Hall of Fame
You understood this basic truth,
    That baseball's just a game.

The game of life counted with you.
    To know you was a pleasure.
Farewell, we love you, Johnny.
    You're a Red Sox treasure.

Fenway Park, Boston, Massachusetts

B54

A Fenway Park postcard from the old days. Not much different today.
(Memorabilia from the Collection of Richard Johnson.)

Williams, DiMaggio, Doerr, and Pesky. Teammates, then, now, and forever. *(Courtesy of the Boston Red Sox.)*

THE TEAMMATES
c. 2010

Dominic, Pesky, Williams and Doerr;

Teammates long ago and forevermore.

The team was the Red Sox. They were its core.

They played as one unit though there were four.

Their team was what mattered, that's how they kept score.

They lived the same way for six decades more.

Teammates then, teammates now, their names etched in lore,

Dominic, Pesky, Williams and Doerr.

PART 5

THE PLAYERS

Casey Stengel, who managed the New York Yankees to five consecutive World Series championships in the 1950s, famously said, "I couldn't have done it without the players." As in most things baseball, Casey was right.

Nothing happens without the players. Games cannot even be held, much less won or lost, without them. That goes for little leagues, major leagues and everything in between.

The players are the game.

Their heroics, their failures and their constant struggle to succeed against the odds are what draw us in to them and to the game. Some, of course, are better than others. There are stars at every level but that is no guarantee that they will successfully reach the next rung on the ladder. There are those who blossom as the challenges become greater, and those impressive minor leaguers who never make it to the big time. We fall in love with some players and we fall out of love with others. But they are the reason that we stay in love with baseball.

Pedro Martinez, baseball's Mozart on the mound.
(Courtesy of the Boston Red Sox.)

BASEBALL'S MOZART

c. 2015

You may talk of baseball stars

In your living rooms and bars,

Debating on by whom you're most impressed.

But I'll say, for what it's worth,

That in all my years on earth

A pitcher we called Pedro was the best.

When a hitter dug right in

He'd feel high heat by his chin

Then wave at a changeup by the knees,

Or a curveball on the paint,

Pedro threw them where they ain't.

And batter after batter faced the squeeze.

He'd put K's up on the board

As his vict'ry total soared.

It is a fact that Pedro reigned supreme.

If a player gave him sass

He'd knock him on his . . . as a matter of fact he wasn't afraid
    to pitch inside.
It was fun as long as he was on your team.
He made every game a show
With the stuff that he would throw.
There is no one any better you can name.
Each pitch was a work of art.
He is baseball's own Mozart.
All hail Pedro Martinez, Hall of Fame.

A 1957 grandstand ticket. They weren't hard to come by back then.
(Memorabilia from the Collection of Richard Johnson.)

David Ortiz, the king of clutch hitters.
(Courtesy of the Boston Red Sox.)

BIG PAPI'S BOMBS

c. 2013

Start carving the statue; get the site ready
Right on the sidewalk between Yaz and Teddy.
He's King of Clutch Hitters; fit him for the crown.
Get driving instructions to old Cooperstown.
He's our Hall of Famer, he'll get there with ease.
The Pope will proclaim him Saint David Ortiz.
To us he's Big Papi; we love it that way.
The big pop's in his bat when he saves the day.
All other teams fear him, from East to West Coast.
He launches those big bombs when it matters most.
On the day that he is installed in the Hall
Sox Nation will be there; his fans, one and all.
And when the Hall plaque is put into his reach
We'll pray that he won't launch F-bombs in his speech.

Dustin Pedroia, our own jumping jock.
(Courtesy of the Boston Red Sox.)

THE JUMPING JOCK
c. 2010

Dustin Pedroia, when playing defense,
Does something strange, yet it also makes sense.
As soon as the pitcher lets the ball go
Pedey jumps up in the air, don't you know.
It's not like he's trying a basketball dunk,
Still, it's a leap with a whole lot of spunk.
When the pitch gets where the batter is standing,
That's the instant Pedroia is landing.
Then, if he should swing and the ball he should meet,
There's Dustin, knees bent, on the balls of his feet.
Wherever it is that the batted ball goes
Pedroia is ready, right on his toes.
He jumps on each pitch in game after game,
But sometimes the jump is not quite the same.
When a knuckle ball's thrown Pedroia could tire.
For the pitch goes so slow that he has to jump higher.
And should the guy balk, well, that's just not fair.
The poor guy gets left hanging up in the air.
He's a leaping jackrabbit, a bouncing-ball hawk.
He's Dustin Pedroia, our own jumping jock.

Carl Yastrzemski, a player like that deserves his own ode.
(Courtesy of the Boston Red Sox.)

RHYMING YASTRZEMSKI

c. 2003

Carl Yastrzemski,
> He wore number eight;
In the field and at bat,
> My God, he was great.

For twenty-three years
> He carried the load.
A player like that
> Deserves his own ode.

But here is the rub.
> Yastrzemski won't rhyme
With any word I
> Have been able to find.

I've lain awake nights,
> I've done the research,

But found not one rhyme.
> I'm left in the lurch.

There just is no rhyme
> To go with Yastrzemski.

And take that from one
> Who's made the attempt-ski.

A 1977 pocket schedule.
(Memorabilia from the Collection of Richard Johnson.)

Yaz, the workingman's hero.
(Courtesy of the Boston Red Sox.)

THE WORKINGMAN'S HERO
c. 2012

There's a name for a man who strove every day,
Persevered at his craft, showed others the way.
There's a name for a man who never would rest,
Who honed all his skills until he was best.
There's a name for a man who made himself great.
The workingman's hero, he wore number eight.
It's a Hall of Fame name, great glory it has.
There's a name for that man—the man known as Yaz.

The class of '14—Roger Clemens, Joe Castiglione, Pedro Martinez, and Nomar Garciaparra. *(Courtesy of the Boston Red Sox.)*

THE CLASS OF '14
c. 2014

When the Red Sox Hall of Fame history's written
With the class of 'fourteen the crowd will be smitten.
Each one will be recognized by his first name,
Such was the impact he had on the game.
They lit up the old ballpark. They put on a show.
They're Pedro and Rocket and Nomar and Joe.
On those games when Pedro would take to the mound
The Great Wall of Fenway would shake from the sound.
His pitches would blaze and they'd bend and they'd dart.
Every one was a great work of art.
We called him the Rocket. Those fastballs he flung
Won as many Sox games as did Cy Young.
He rose to each challenge; his veins were like ice.
Twenty strikeouts a game; and he did it twice.
He tugged on his gloves, tapped his toes just a tad,
He was the best shortstop the Sox ever had.
His fielding was peerless, his bat beyond par.

Sox Nation loved him. He was our "No-mah."
Describing their glory as each would achieve it
Was Joe on the radio. Can you believe it?
The class of 'fourteen in the Sox Hall of Fame;
We know their exploits. We know them by name.
We'll never forget them. Their legends will grow.
They're Pedro and Rocket and Nomar and Joe.

TO THE PLAYERS

c. 2008

Here's to you, Tom Brunansky,
      Bruce Hurst and Mel Parnell,
To Rico Petrocelli,
      Mike Timlin, Gary Bell,
Let's not forget Bill Monbouquette,
      Rich Gedman or Sam Mele,
Or Ellis Burks, or Rudy York,
      Mo Vaughn or Aaron Sele.
To Pumpsie Green and Sammy White,
      Trot Nixon and Butch Hobson.
To Jimmy Piersall, Oil Can Boyd,
      Mike Greenwell and Joe Dobson.
Marty Barrett, Reggie Smith,
      Ted Lepcio, Bill Lee,
And Jackie Jensen, Wilbur Wood,
      Bob Stanley, Roy Partee.

To Tommy Harper, Billy Rohr,
Walt Dropo, Cecil Cooper.
To Brian Daubach, Pokey Reese,
Mike Andrews, Harry Hooper.
A bow to Dennis Eckersley,
To Wade Boggs and Joe Foy.
To all of those who played the game
That's given us such joy.
They hit, they pitched, they ran, they threw,
They gave our souls a lift.
They brought baseball into our lives
And that's a great, great gift.

IT'S A GREAT DAY FOR THE RED SOX
c. 2007

It's a great day for the Red Sox
They're Irish to a man
Varitek and Youkilis are both from Kerry
Big Papi, he's got a place in Tipperary

It's a great day for Ramirez
He's Irish by the way
We're feeling so insp-irish
Matsuzaka's also Irish
It's a great, great day!

It's a great day for the Red Sox
The team's all wearing green
Schilling, Crisp and Papelbon are filled with Blarney
Mirabelli is a Kelly from Killarney

It's a great day for Francona
I think he's from Galway
They've got Irish bosses we know
They're named Epstein and Lucchino
It's a great, great day!

Manny Ramirez—how did we solve the problem that was Manny?
(Courtesy of the Boston Red Sox.)

THE MANNY SONG

(To the tune of "Maria (The Nun Song)"
from the musical The Sound of Music)

c. 2008

How did we solve the problem that was Manny?
Trying to figure him out kept us awake.
How could we know that Manny needed a nanny?
A hitting machine, but out of his bean, a flake.

Many a time we'd like to strangle Manny.
Many a time he played the role of a clown.
He simply disgusted us all
By peeing inside of the Wall
Then the fly in his pants would still be down.

Oh, how did we solve the problem that was Manny?
We gave him a one-way ticket out of town.

A Red Sox Comedy

HASTY PUDDING THEATRE

Program from a comedy about the Red Sox. It could have just as easily been a tragedy.
(Memorabilia from the Collection of Richard Johnson.)

HAIL TO JOHN FARRELL

(To the tune of "Roll Out the Barrel")

c. 2013

Hail to John Farrell, the Red Sox' great managing star.
We know, John Farrell, you're best in all baseball by far.
Cheers for John Farrell, you've brought us a barrel of wins.
Everybody loves John Farrell,
At least 'til next season begins.

Good show, John Farrell, you won us a World Series crown.
We're pro–John Farrell, we're faithful. We won't let you down.
We love John Farrell, but we would like you to know
We could turn on you, John Farrell,
When you lose ten games in a row.

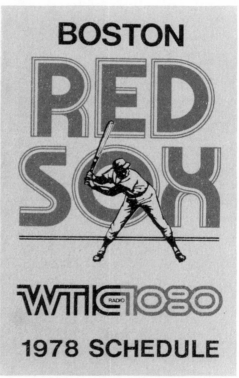

A pocket schedule from 1978.
*(Memorabilia from the Collection
of Richard Johnson.)*

JOHN FARRELL'S MEN

*(With apologies to Sigmund Romberg and
Oscar Hammerstein)*

c. 2013

Give me some men who are John Farrell's men
And you'll soon hear a World Series roar

Start me with nine and a bullpen that's fine
And then runs by the tons they will score

B's on their hats and with thunderous bats
They'll be champs to enhance our folklore

There's no way the Sox cannot fulfill our dream
When John Farrell's men repeat as our
World Champion Team.

Jackie Robinson—one man can make a difference.
(*Courtesy of National Baseball Hall of Fame Library, Cooperstown, NY.*)

JACKIE ROBINSON
c. 2002

He often said down through the years
  He never had it made.
He was tested, he was taunted,
  In every game he played.

Not just on the field of play,
  But in the game of life.
He knew very well the feel
  Of prejudice and strife.

He was on a baseball team,
  And yet, he was alone.
The very first black player
  The major leagues had known.

All eyes were upon him.
  Many wanted him to fail.
The pressure was enormous,
  For he knew he must prevail.

The racial slurs and insults flew,
  And, yes, he heard them all.
But he summoned all his strength to keep
  His eye upon the ball.

Centuries of bigotry,
  That's what he would attack.
He took the country with him,
  Put us upon his back.

He was more than good enough.
  Oh, how he played the game.
His running and his hitting;
  First ballot, Hall of Fame.

Because of him the racist walls
  Came tumbling to the ground.
Now players of all colors
  On every team are found.

One man can make a difference,
  For when all is said and done,
This game, this land, they're better
  Thanks to Jackie Robinson.

A Ladies Day ticket stub—twenty-five
cents got you into the park.
*(Memorabilia from the Collection of
Richard Johnson.)*

Mariano Rivera—Were he not a Yankee he'd rate an A-plus.
(Courtesy of the Boston Red Sox.)

GOOD LUCK, MARIANO
c. 2013

I have to admit that I get the crankies

When somebody mentions the Damn New York Yankees.

I just do not like them. It's one of my gripes.

They strut around wearing their fancy pinstripes.

There is one exception, someone I don't blame.

A prince of a fellow; Rivera's his name.

He's top-notch; a class act, the finest you'll meet.

He helps sweet old ladies while crossing the street.

You can't help but like him, although he's a foe.

He's a wonderful guy. He's Mariano.

In closing out ballgames, well, it's understood

He's the best of all time. The guy is that good.

He's saved games forever. To tell you the truth,

I think that he played with both Gehrig and Ruth.

Were he not a Yankee he'd rate an A-plus.

Good luck, Mariano. But not against us.

Derek Jeter—a heck of a player who wore the wrong laundry.
(Courtesy of the Boston Red Sox.)

FARE THEE WELL, DEREK JETER
c. 2014

For the past twenty years we've been in a quandary.
A heck of a player has worn the wrong laundry.
We've rooted against him, but this is a fact,
Except for those pinstripes the guy's a class act.
We like and respect him and let it be said
We'd have liked him much more if his socks had been red.
There've been dozens of times he's ruined our plans
With a timely base hit, a dive into the stands.
Oh, we've won our share on many a night
But with him on the field we were in for a fight.
It's been best of both worlds, for now we can say
That we root for the Sox but we saw Jeter play.
Fare thee well, Derek Jeter; adios, happy walks.
To remember us by here's a pair of Red Sox!

TO THE HALL OF FAMERS
c. 2014

Here's to you, Teddy Williams,
          Babe Ruth and Rube Waddell,
To Cy Young, Walter Johnson,
          Satch Paige, Cool Papa Bell.
Greg Maddux, Tommy Glavine,
          Frank Thomas, Bobby Cox.
Tony La Russa, Connie Mack,
          Joe Torre, Jimmie Foxx.
Yogi Berra, Johnny Bench
          And to Roy Campanella,
Nolan Ryan, Whitey Ford
          And Rapid Robert Feller.
To Warren Spahn and Arky Vaughan,
          Stan Musial, Lou Boudreau,
To Willie Mays, Tris Speaker
          And Joe DiMaggio,
Early Wynn and Tony Gwynn,

Hank Aaron and Pie Traynor,
Rogers Hornsby, Bobby Doerr
And to the brothers Waner.
Mickey Mantle, Ernie Banks,
Lou Gehrig and Tom Seaver.
Jackie Robinson, Pudge Fisk,
Let's not forget Earl Weaver,
Ducky Medwick, Dizzy Dean,
Duke Snider, Dazzy Vance,
Sandy Koufax, Al Kaline,
To Tinker, Evers, Chance.
A bow to Carl Yastrzemski,
Mel Ott, Three Finger Brown.
They all played the game so well
That they're in Cooperstown.
To all whose plaques are in the Hall,
The legends they became.
They were the best at what they did,
True artists of the game.

SANDOVAL IS COMING TO TOWN
c. 2014

You better watch out, 'cause this is no lie.
The Red Sox are back. I'm telling you why.
Sandoval is coming to town.

He's playing third base, we'll be in first place;
He's such a big star with such a big waist.
Sandoval is coming to town.

The Panda Bear's on our side,
Hanley Ramirez, too.
If other teams say they're the best
We will simply say, "Kung fu."

He's got a great glove, he's got a great bat,
You've got to admit the guy's really fabulous!
Sandoval is coming to town.

The cart that ferried pitchers from the bullpen.
It's still on display in the park.
*(Memorabilia from the Collection of
Richard Johnson.)*

Nobody loves a baseball umpire. *(Courtesy of National Baseball Hall of Fame Library, Cooperstown, NY.)*

THE UMPIRE
c. 2012

I bring you sad news, in fact, even dire.

Nobody loves a baseball umpire.

Such universal lack of affection

Has to result in a sense of rejection.

Neither team trusts him, he makes their skin crawl.

One side will be mad whatever his call.

If it's against you the bum is a crook.

And if you agree he's just a poor schnook.

He's an object of scorn, someone we all shun.

But the poor devil is some mother's son.

So remember before he screws up the next pitch

That every umpire's a son of a—person who probably isn't too
   crazy about him or herself.

PART 6

BEHIND THE CURTAIN

In baseball the team on the field is the end product. The team in the front office is the engine that produces it. Just as *The Wizard of Oz* had a man behind the curtain, so does every other organization, including baseball.

When new ownership took control of the Red Sox in 2002 it marked a change in culture—and in results—for the entire organization. Those at the top pooled their talents to become a uniquely effective combination: Principal owner John Henry, the high-tech genius and entrepreneur whose knowledge and understanding of numbers is unparalleled; Chairman Tom Werner, television innovator and former owner of the San Diego Padres; and President and Chief Executive Officer Larry Lucchino, the hard-driving wagon master who cares so much about the organization and who cares even more about his people. All possess different but complementary skills and all share a common passion for the game. To the mix they added other key elements, including Dr. Charles Steinberg, the dentist who became the maestro of the fan experience and who has never lost the mentality of a young boy in love with baseball.

Three World Series championships later and well into the second decade of its stewardship the group is still collectively known among Bostonians as the "new" ownership. That might last awhile. After all, in Boston there is a building at the crest of Beacon Hill that first opened its doors in 1798 and natives still refer to it as the "new" statehouse.

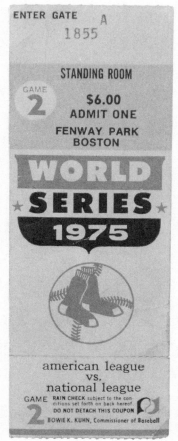

A 1975 World Series ticket. It was still only six bucks for standing room. *(Memorabilia from the Collection of Richard Johnson.)*

John Henry, Red Sox majority owner—the whole town's MVP.
(Courtesy of the Boston Red Sox.)

ODE TO JOHN HENRY
c. 2005

John Henry, you're a leader,
     You broke the dreaded curse.
We suffered for so many years,
     Things couldn't get much worse.

We'd come so close to victory
     Then out the door it went
The ball would go through someone's legs,
     Or Bucky "Bleeping" Dent.

Then you came upon the scene
     And, John, you saved the day.
You knew that winning means much more
     Than on the field of play.

Oh sure, you built a baseball team,
     One that is for the ages.

They can pitch and they can hit.
>You pay them damn good wages.

But it's what you've done for everyone
>Through your Red Sox Foundation.
You've brought us all together
>In this place called Red Sox Nation.

You've helped the sick, you've helped the poor.
>Brought racial harmony.
And that's why we salute you, John.
>You're the whole town's MVP.

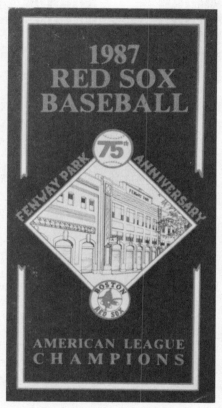

A Red Sox schedule for 1987.
*(Memorabilia from the Collection
of Richard Johnson.)*

Larry Lucchino, Red Sox president and CEO—the man who must feed the savage beast—us! *(Courtesy of the Boston Red Sox.)*

A HYMN TO LARRY

(To the tune of "When You and I Were Young, Maggie")

c. 2006

I wandered today to the park, Larry,
My gosh, the place looks great.
And on it you have left your mark, Larry,
The changes have all turned out first-rate.
The Green Monster seats in left field, Larry,
The EMC Club behind home plate,
They not only have a great feel, Larry,
They all mean more money at the gate.

Your eye's on the old bottom line, Larry,
John Henry sends his thanks.
Oh gee, everything would be fine, Larry,
If we could just beat the bleeping Yanks.
The media's all on your back, Larry,
Sox Nation is out for blood I fear.
But you can throw them off the track, Larry,
Just tell them to wait until next year.

Dr. Charles Steinberg, Red Sox executive vice president—the
Maestro of Fenway Park. *(Courtesy of the Boston Red Sox.)*

ODE TO DR. CHARLES
c. 2014

Doctor Charles, we love ya.
> You're top-notch, you're the Man!

You've made it extra special
> To be a Red Sox fan.

You're the Maestro, the bandleader,
> The Man Behind the Curtain.

You've made each game a work of art.
> That's a fact, for certain.

From pregame ceremonies
> To videos and songs

You've enriched baseball enjoyment
> For all those Fenway throngs.

You've reached out to communities,
> You've helped each neighborhood.

You've given everything you've got
    To causes that are good.

Not bad for a dentist.
        You've earned a laurel wreath.
But getting you to take a bow
        Is just like pulling teeth.

But now you're in our clutches,
        So we'll get this off our chest:
We're grateful for all you have done,
        For, Charles, you are the best!

RAIN CHECK ADMISSION STUB

GRANDSTAND

ADMISSION **$2.75**

If legal game is not played or not rescheduled with this same ticket valid, this rain check may be exchanged at box office for a ticket of the same price, if available, for any future regularly scheduled American League game of the current season.

NO MONEY REFUNDED

BOSTON RED SOX

SEC.	ROW	SEAT
17	8	3

DATE

June 5 1971

RAIN CHECK 10105

A good seat in 1971 cost two dollars and seventy-five cents. *(Memorabilia from the Collection of Richard Johnson.)*

Lou Gorman, former general manager—we were lucky to have known him. *(Courtesy of the Boston Red Sox.)*

WE MISS YOU, LOU
c. 2011

He loved the game of baseball
      And he loved his fellow man.
He treated all with dignity,
      Each player, stranger, fan.

He spent his lifetime building teams.
      He knew the heights of glory.
He knew the ballgame inside out,
      And could he tell a story.

When things went wrong (they sometimes did),
      That's when he really shone.
He protected those around him
      And bore the brunt alone.

He never bent, he never wavered;
      Didn't whimper, didn't scream.

He took the slings and arrows
    And he did it for the team.

He was proud to be a Navy man,
    A Stonehill College grad.
No greater benefactor
    Those places ever had.

It was grand to just be with him,
    To stand next to where he stood.
He made you feel important,
    Or, as he would say, "Good, good."

We were lucky to have known him
    And the game was lucky, too.
He was unlike any other.
    So long, we miss you, Lou.

PART 7

FOR THE LOVE
OF THE GAME

In 2004, graves throughout New England and beyond were bedecked with memorabilia from the Red Sox World Series victory. In places like Boston, where baseball has been a deep-rooted part of the culture for a century and more, the love for it has become a part of our legacy, passed on from generation to generation. So when the eighty-six-year Red Sox drought finally ended, it was cause for celebration, even with the long departed.

For so many of us baseball is a lifelong companion. We fall in love with it in our early grammar school years and it stays by our side ever after, through the coming-of-age years, marriages, the birth of children, working lives and on into retirement and the sunset years. The game has changed, just as all of us have, but at its core it remains the same; it's still ninety feet from home to first, sixty feet six inches from the pitching rubber to home plate, and the hardest thing in sports is still hitting a round ball squarely with a round bat when it's coming at you at speeds of ninety-five miles an hour and more.

Baseball enriches us, inspires us, frustrates us and sometimes angers us, but it is always there. The players who play it are not perfect. The moguls who run it are not perfect. Some of our fellow fans are an embarrassment. Games and entire seasons can turn into disasters, vast wastelands filled with disappointment and despair.

But there is always next year.

And there is always baseball.

A patch from the 1916 World Series champs.
(Memorabilia from the Collection of Richard Johnson.)

The magic of Opening Day.
(Courtesy of the Boston Red Sox.)

OPENING DAY
c. 2013

The long barren winter casts a dark pall
Till one day an umpire hollers, "Play ball!"
Then skies start to brighten, blue displaces gray.
Baseball springs eternal. It's Opening Day.
The birds begin singing. The trees start to bloom.
The umpire's dusting home plate with his broom.
No one's thrown a pitch yet, or failed to reach base,
But everyone's team's in a tie for first place.
They're all undefeated. They all have a chance.
We all dream of doing a World Series dance.
The setbacks will surface, the losses, the gloom.
Each team except one is destined for doom.
But our guys might win it, so let's start to play.
And that is the magic of Opening Day.

When you first discover baseball, when you're given
your first glove. *(Courtesy of the Boston Red Sox.)*

TO BE IN LOVE WITH BASEBALL
c. 2006

When you first discover baseball,
    When you're given your first glove,
You find out at a tender age
    What it's like to fall in love.

You learn to play; you learn the rules;
    What the game's about.
There are three outs in each inning;
    It's three strikes and you're out.

When first you see a big-league park,
    Those stands, that field of green,
You know as long as you shall live
    You won't forget that scene.

So you root for the old home team,
    A favorite player choose,

And you learn life's hardest lesson:

      There are lots of times you lose.

Then you realize your parents

      And your grandfather, too,

All have this in common,

      They love it just like you.

And seven decades down the road

      That love is still the same.

For all the memories you have

      What counts is the next game.

For your whole life it's part of you.

      Its praises must be sung.

For to be in love with baseball

      Is to be forever young.

AN UPDATED ANTHEM
c. 2014

Take me out to the ballgame.
First, let's stop at the bank.
I'll need a mortgage so I can pay.
Parking the car is another outlay.
And you pay big bucks for a hot dog,
The cost for beer is insane.
For it's Oh my! Prices are high
At the old ballgame.

Trucking on down to Spring Training in Fort Myers, Florida.
(Courtesy of the Boston Red Sox.)

TRUCK DAY
c. 2013

There's light at the end of the tunnel.
> Spring training is not far away.
The truck is all loaded and ready.
> Fort Myers, it's heading your way.

Soon it will be in the sunshine
> While we're up here freezing, you know.
Perhaps you could do us a favor
> And load up the darn thing with snow.

This winter has dragged on forever,
> Enough with this Frozen Fenway.
Get trucking on down to spring training.
> We're ready for baseball, I'd say.

Bon voyage, adios, see you later.
> Make tracks, move it out, on your way.
When you come back bring sunny weather.
> And be here by Opening Day.

1967—to dream the Impossible Dream, winning the American League pennant. *(Courtesy of the Boston Red Sox.)*

'67 AND THE BOSOX CLUB
c. 2002

Listen, Sox Nation, and you shall hear
About 'sixty-seven, one hell of a year.
It began with the team in a terrible fix
They'd finished in ninth place in 'sixty-six.

But a bunch of Sox diehards here in the Hub
Refused to lose faith, so they formed a new club.
The BoSox Club started and set a great precedent
When Dom DiMaggio became its first president.

People joined up with Dom's name on the door,
Now all they lacked was a team to root for.
Then the season began and that little-known team
Set out to achieve the impossible dream.

They gave us more thrills than any team has
With Lonborg and Rico and the man they called Yaz.

Folks here in Boston recall 'sixty-seven
As the greatest of all, the season from heaven.

The year that fulfilled a long-suffering thirst
When the Red Sox traveled from ninth place to first.
And the BoSox Club has gone on to expand
Into the greatest fan club in the land.

So, Red Sox Nation, do not despair,
There's another miracle out there somewhere.
When things don't go well and the future looks blue,
Remember, the Impossible Dream can come true.

Another Red Sox pennant. Who knew?
(Memorabilia from the Collection of Richard Johnson.)

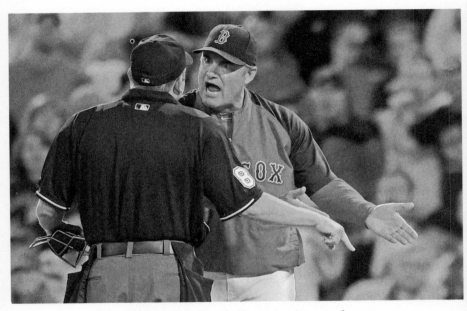

There's nothing in baseball you can't second-guess.
(Courtesy of the Boston Red Sox.)

SECOND-GUESSING
c. 2008

There's this about baseball that's truly a blessing:
It's a barrel of fun if you like second-guessing.
You can sit in the stands or at home in a chair
Manager bashing, lambasting a player.
You can pick apart lineups, critique every switch.
"Send up a pinch hitter," "Don't let that bum pitch."
"Hold up the runner." "Send him in to score."
"The guy took strike three." "He swung at ball four."
"Get rid of that pitcher." "We need a new bat."
"Please tell me why we can't get guys like that."
"The umpire's blind. He just called that a strike."
"Ketchup on hot dogs. Now, that I don't like."
No one pays attention, but nevertheless
There's nothing in baseball you can't second-guess.
But I'm telling you this and I'll say it out flat,
It's the best game of all. Now second-guess that!

Why doesn't a passed ball count as an error?
(Courtesy of the Boston Red Sox.)

PET PEEVES
c. 2009

Here is a puzzle to stump Yogi Berra.
Why doesn't a passed ball count as an error?
A guy lets a pitched ball go right through his hands
Allowing all runners on base to advance.
Write it down as an error in pen and ink.
Same thing for wild pitches. That's what I think.
Or, a guy hits a ground ball to drive in a run.
He's charged with an at bat, the son of a gun.
But it's not an at bat if the ball's in the air.
It's a sacrifice fly. That doesn't seem fair.
And while I am at it this makes me sore,
What in the world is the coach's box for?
Don't coaches belong there through the whole game?
Sometimes they're out where the zip code's not the same.
These things are upsetting, they leave quite a scar,
As does forgetting where I parked the car.
But I'm feeling much better with this off my chest.
Now if you'll excuse me I'll lie down and rest.

PART 8

THE RED SOX
AND ME

Baseball is something all its fans have in common, yet each of us has his or her own personal memories and experiences with the game. Some of mine are recounted here. I once actually got up to bat at Fenway Park, not in a game but at a charity event, and I faced a machine, not a real pitcher. Still, I was up there. When I was a kid a friend and I concocted an ill-advised scheme to start a phony fan club for Red Sox pitcher Ellis Kinder. Former Dodger general manager Tommy Lasorda, apparently unhappy after being outshone at the banquet the previous night, once refused to introduce me at an event for the Ted Williams Museum and Hitters Hall of Fame at which I was scheduled to recite "Teddy at the Bat." When former Sox manager Theo Epstein once temporarily quit his job I daydreamed about running the club myself.

The old man and the bat. My futility at the plate was
matched only by my inability to run, field, or throw.
(Courtesy of the Boston Red Sox.)

THE OLD MAN AND THE BAT
c. 2010

'Twas a balmy summer morning
     And a paltry crowd was there
In fact, the stands were empty
     In the park near Kenmore Square.

But some folks for charity
     Stood in there at home plate.
They batted versus a machine
     The results were hardly great.

Then an old man standing in their midst
     Stepped up and grabbed a bat.
He said, "I'll show you how it's done."
     And into his hand he spat.

He took his stance on hallowed ground
     Where the Babe and Ted had stood.

Then he remembered as a kid
    He wasn't very good.

In fact, as he thought back on it
    The mem'ry of it hurt.
He'd never hit a single ball
    Beyond the infield dirt.

His swing was still as feeble,
    His mechanics just as poor.
He was every bit as lousy
    As in days of yore.

Then he was down to his last swing,
    His last shot, do or die.
Could he get ahold of one?
    By golly, he would try.

Sure enough, in came the heat
    At, maybe, fifty per.
He uncorked a mighty swing,
    His bat was just a blur.

He hit that fastball squarely
    And unleashed a mighty blast
It landed just beyond the dirt
    But in the outfield grass.

He'd never done that as a lad
    And now he'd hit one longer.
The old man thought with passing years
    He must be getting stronger.

Beyond a doubt now, he's convinced,
    If he can stay alive,
He might reach the Pesky Pole
    By the time he's ninety-five.

At last it can be told, the secret story of Ellis Kinder's phantom fan club. *(Courtesy of the Boston Red Sox.)*

MY DARK SECRET
c. 2011

We all have dark secrets that nobody knows.
This is my confession. You ready? Here it goes.
For years I've avoided arrest and conviction
For starting a fan club that was a pure fiction.
In the pages of *Sport* magazine it was listed.
But the truth is the darn thing never existed.
Ellis Kinder was a Sox pitcher of note,
It was he in whose name I floated the boat.
I figured I could sidestep any blame
By simply signing another kid's name.
But here's my mistake, I don't think I should
Have told everyone in the whole neighborhood.
That kid's father told me I had, by God,
Used the United States Mail to defraud.
Of Kinder's wrath I don't have any fears.
Ellis has been dead for forty-three years.
But I haven't slept well to this very day.

The Feds might show up to take me away.
I had an accomplice. It wasn't just me,
But guess what? That guy just got away free.
Here's how the guy has avoided detection.
He joined a program called Witness Protection.

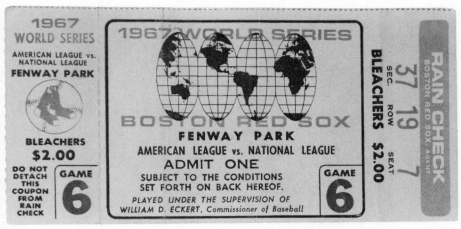

A seat in the bleachers for the 1967 World Series.
(Memorabilia from the Collection of Richard Johnson.)

Tommy Lasorda—same to you, Tommy.
(Courtesy of the Boston Red Sox.)

TOMMY, HOW COULD YOU?
c. 2002

Oh, Tommy, how could you? Please say it ain't so,
That someone like you would do something so low.
There I was in the lineup, all ready to speak.
But you wouldn't let me, you scoundrel, you sneak.
As I blissfully sat there up on the stand
On my introduction, Tommy, you fanned.
Don't say you forgot me, that isn't the case
Tom, you deliberately left me on base.
Were you just afraid that I might get a laugh?
Is that why, you rascal, you gave me the shaft?
You're full of it, Tommy, and I'm telling you
The "it" that you're full of is not Dodger blue.

If Theo Epstein quits his present job, I'll apply for that, too.
(Courtesy of the Boston Red Sox.)

A JOB APPLICATION
c. 2005

Today I'm announcing, excuse me, ahem,
That I'm seeking the job of the Red Sox GM.
Here's why I think I should get it, you see.
Unlike that guy Theo, I'll do it for free.
His age, my IQ, they're exactly the same
I just want to get in to see every game.
Just give me two seats for each game that they play.
I'll scalp 'em and make several million that way.
I'll be a fan favorite, on that you can bet.
I'm taking charm lessons from a guy named Duquette.
So I'm asking you, please, this message to carry
In case you should happen to run into Larry.
He'll choose me I know if I get this across,
I'm like Scooter Libby. I'll lie for the boss!

Mrs. Flavin's youngest boy, Richard.
(Courtesy of the Boston Red Sox.)

THE SKINNY ON ME
c. 2009

Here's the skinny on this Flavin guy,
  The one who writes the poesy.
He's Mrs. Flavin's youngest boy.
  She loved him head to toesy.
His commentaries on TV
  Gave politicians hives.
The set designers way back then
  Were Currier and Ives.
He skewered parties equally,
  Republicans and Demmies.
And got away with so much
  That he won seven Emmys.
He wrote a play on Tip O'Neill,
  Revealing and quite funny.
It brought him fame and some acclaim
  And everything but money.
He writes ditties on the Red Sox,

Their victories and losses.
He'll even rhyme from time to time
    To tweak the BoSox bosses.
He'll give a speech in your hometown.
    He'll do the speaking tour.
Truth is, if it comes to that,
    He'll go from door to door.
He's fooled some folks some of the time
    By doing all that stuff.
And that, he's very pleased to say,
    Seems to be quite enough.

ACKNOWLEDGMENTS

This little book could never have happened without the Boston Red Sox, with whom I have been in love all my life. The team on the field might have let me down on more than one occasion over the past seven decades but the present-day organization has never wavered in its enthusiastic support of me and of this book. Starting from the top, Larry Lucchino and Sam Kennedy have been exceedingly generous and that has spread throughout the entire shop. Charles Steinberg is my Red Sox rabbi. He has been my biggest booster and my most trusted confidante. Pam Kenn has helped in countless ways. The late Dick Bresciani provided invaluable guidance, as he did for so many others. Thanks to Sarah Coffin, Michael Ivins, Billy Weiss, Dave Friedman and Dave Beeston.

At William Morrow Lisa Sharkey has been my champion—for that I am grateful—and Daniella Valladares, my editor, has guided me with a steady and patient hand and constant good cheer.

Nobody in or around baseball has earned more respect than the estimable Peter Gammons and I am in his debt for his writing the foreword.

Donna Cohen has led me through the labyrinth of business and legal issues that are beyond my comprehension. She is a great pro and a great dame. Billie Munro Audia and Karen Zahler have been of invaluable help. Harry Sherr set the wheels in motion to get this project off the ground and Gary and Lynne Smith have championed it from the start. I am thankful to Richard Johnson, curator of the Sports Museum of New England, for generously allowing the use of memorabilia from his personal collection.

I am thankful to George Mitrovich, chairman of the Great Fenway Park Writers Series; the BoSox Club, the official booster club of the Red Sox; and the Blohards, a New York City–based group of Red Sox fanatics (and they say that only the game fish swims upstream!). All have happily allowed the use of their venues to test out and hone material.

Finally, my thanks to Ernest Lawrence Thayer, who could not have known back in 1888, when he wrote a humorous poem for the *San Francisco Examiner* called "Casey at the Bat," that it would one day lead to this.